MEASURE:
Adventures at
Prosperity Patch

by Kim D. H. Butler
and Spencer Shaw

MEASURE: Adventures at Prosperity Patch
Copyright © 2025 Kim D. H. Butler and Spencer Shaw

Prosperity Economics Movement
22790 Highway 259 South
Mount Enterprise, TX 75681
www.ProsperityEconomics.org

First Edition
ISBN: 979-8-9940994-1-4 (paperback)

Produced in the United States of America

Published with the assistance of Social Motion Publishing, which specializes in books that benefit causes and nonprofits. For more information, go to SocialMotionPublishing.com.

Acknowledgments

I love animals; I have had dogs, cats, chickens, pigs, sheep, goats, and dairy cows since 4th grade, and now I have Alpacas! I also love Prosperity Thinking. Now, I am excited to share these loves with children of all ages through my third love: reading! Whether you are an adult or have children, grandchildren, or great-grandchildren, reading with others (and playing games too!) is a fabulous bonding experience, and I am so grateful to the team of Spencer and family for bringing it to your table.

Enjoy, Kim Butler, Mount Enterprise, TX

I grew up hearing stories from my dad and kinfolk which shaped my world today. Sharing stories with kids is a fun way to help them think about big dreams. Huge thank you to my wife for leading our homeschooling and our kids for listening to these stories. A big thank you to Emma for helping Kim and I feel like children again.

We are so grateful to everyone who helps us make this book, like Amanda who leads this project and our awesome designers Cy and Holly.

Spencer Shaw

Peanut the Cat stretched out of bed from his midmorning snooze and found an old, faded map hidden in a dusty corner of the barn.

It was a treasure map, promising hidden treats and toys buried somewhere on the farm. Excitement quickly spread among the pets.

Gathered in the barn, Emma, Peanut, Zippy, Miguel, and Kid imagined what fun and games awaited them. Each pet dreamed of the adventure and the treasures that might be found.

However, Emma, the wise Great Dane, called everyone to circle around. "Before we go looking for treasure, let's think about what we'll miss doing today," she said, her voice calm and caring. "We need to decide if searching for treasure is worth skipping our other fun plans."

The pets paused to think. Miguel had planned to fix the fence, but it could wait a day. Zippy had a playdate, which he could reschedule. Peanut was supposed to organize the barn, but it wasn't urgent. Kid thought about the nap he'd miss but decided an adventure was more exciting.

Understanding what they might miss out on, the pets agreed that the chance for an adventure was too good to pass up. They voted and decided together to follow the map and seek the treasure, excited about the journey ahead.

They set off with the map in paw, following the clues across the fields and through the woods. They crossed streams and climbed hills, their laughter echoing through the air.

As the sun began to set, they reached the spot marked on the map. Digging eagerly, they uncovered a small chest. Inside were some old farm toys and a note that read, "The real treasure is the adventure and the friends you make along the way."

As they shared the toys, they talked about their day. They hadn't found gold or jewels but they had a great time and made memories together.

They learned that some things, like a day of fun with friends, were worth more than what they had given up.

Back at the barn as the stars began to appear in the twilight sky, Emma summed up the day's lesson.

"Today, we learned to think about what we give up when we make choices. We chose adventure today, and it was worth it!"

Emma's Advice:

Making choices is important and helps shape what happens next in your life. Even small choices can change things. When you think carefully about your choices, you learn to be confident and solve problems. Sometimes, if you make quick decisions without thinking, you might feel sorry later. It's okay to make mistakes because they help you learn and make better choices next time. By practicing making choices now, you get ready to handle anything that comes your way!

Emma's Questions:

1. Why do you think it's important to carefully choose which toy to play with first, and how might that affect your playtime?
2. What exciting things do you think might happen if you decide to share your snack with a friend? How do you think it will make them feel?
3. How do you feel when you have to pick between two fun games to play? What do you think helps you make that choice?
4. What interesting things could you discover if you try something new, like tasting a different kind of food? How might that change what you like to eat?
5. How do you decide what to wear when it's cold outside, and why is making the right choice important for keeping you comfortable?

A note for your parents!

As our thank-you, the QR code below will give you a valuable white paper focused on Income Strategies at ProsperityEconomics.org/permission.

www.ingramcontent.com/pod-product-compliance
Lightning Source LLC
Chambersburg PA
CBHW041719200326
41520CB00001B/167